JOINING THE SCOTTISH POLICE FORCE

Scott Dixon

Contents

Introduction

The inspiration behind this book came about after having an interview for a temporary pensions administration role for Police Scotland after I published my book titled *How To Get The Job You Want*.

Whilst I was pipped by someone with specific pensions administration experience, I received excellent feedback as I was well prepared and knew what to expect.

I understand the core competencies and how Police Scotland measure your responses to score your ability to perform in your chosen role. By learning how you are measured and having the answers I gave to the questions I was asked, you will be able to craft your own answers based on your personal experiences.

In September 2016, I wrote and published a consumer book which has plenty of 5* reviews on Amazon and has sold on 3 continents. *How to Complain: The Consumer Guide to Resolve Complaints and Motoring Disputes* spans various consumer laws over 3 jurisdictions (England and Wales, Scotland and the Isle of Man).

The second edition is updated to comply with the latest Data Protection laws that were introduced in May 2018 with new templates for Data Subject Access Requests. It has also been updated as consumer laws and issues are never static with plenty of advice, test cases, real-life examples and templates so you can get results every time with the minimum of fuss.

BBC Radio Scotland and the Daily Mail have featured me as 1 of 5 of the best Consumer Champions in the UK from publishing this book.

My consumer website www.thegrumpygit.com which complements the book attracts plenty of global traffic. You will find over 100 blogs spanning various consumer matters of interest as well as a few random blogs inspired by chance conversations and experiences. The blog is a platform to convey thoughts and musings to a global audience on topics that people find factual, engaging and enjoyable to read.

My job interview book titled *'How To Get The Job You Want and Bin The Job You Hate'* is based on a lifetime of interviews and experiences in the public and private sector and knowing precisely what to expect and how to secure an interview is also available to purchase.

I hope you find this book informative, engaging and an enjoyable read.

Cover Letter

A concise, well written cover letter will set your application apart from other applicants in capturing the attention of your future employer from the outset, and research suggests that you increase your chances by about 47% in securing an interview with a good cover letter.

Every role is different, even within the same organisation, so it is imperative that your cover letter is tailored to suit the specific role you are applying for. This is your opportunity to impress the individual who is vetting the applications before they even read your CV.

Find out who to personally address the letter to rather than a generic 'Dear Sir / Madam' to ensure your application is considered and noticed for the right reasons. This can be found in the job advert or by searches on LinkedIn or Google.

In the first paragraph, state the role that you wish to be considered for and why you are applying for the role.

In the second paragraph, elaborate on why you would like to work for this organisation and convey your knowledge and passion you share, complete with your knowledge of the organisation. A good way to connect with your prospective employer is to express that you share their values and ethos and that you would be a great ambassador in promoting these if you were hired and aspire to exceed their set targets and goals.

You could clearly bullet point the skills, expertise and work experience that the employer requires in this section.

The third paragraph is where you focus on your skills and experience relevant to the job advert. It is paramount that you match your skills to what this role requires as well as the fact that you are adaptable and can easily learn whatever is required to perform effectively in the role.

You can encapsulate the strengths you have gathered throughout your life on a professional and personal level that would add value to the role and business holistically. It is useful to throw in some examples of outside hobbies and interests that capture your strengths at this point, simply to convey that you are a rounded individual who is adaptable and one that fits in well with individuals from all walks of life.

Your final paragraph should wrap up your letter succinctly, thanking your prospective employer for taking the time to read your letter and that you look forward to hearing from them.

One template that I use to craft my cover letters is given below;

Dear X,

I wish to apply for the role of (X) as advertised on your website.

I am familiar with effective time management by virtue of various roles primarily in financial services where I have had to identify and effectively manage risk to time-driven deadlines.

I have a good working knowledge of Word and intermediate Excel skills, which is demonstrated from my work as a professional writer and author in tandem with a popular consumer website I host that attracts plenty of global traffic. I manage my own publishing firm, prepare the accounts and keep the statutory records in good order.

My last role at (firm)... (describe role and responsibilities).

I would relish the opportunity to work with a well-respected organisation and employer of choice that can offer a structured career progression and apply my varied skills set to benefit your organisation and stakeholders.

I am seeking a full-time permanent position and my current salary is £X + benefits with a 1-week notice period.

I would welcome the opportunity to meet you at a mutually convenient time to discuss my CV, and I look forward to hearing from you soon.

Yours sincerely,

Social Media

Current research suggests that 70% of recruiters look at social media profiles of applicants on Facebook and LinkedIn before considering inviting an applicant to an interview and about 43% of employers use social media to check on current employees. A similar number of employers have actually sourced a candidate through social media.

Almost all employers (93% is the figure given) vet applicants via social media during the interview process. Therefore, it's imperative you ensure your profiles project the right impression based on what you post and the type of photos you share; all of which can be found in the public domain.

Employers are looking for candidates who are creative and social and will be screening out those they consider as having inappropriate online behaviour. Whilst that is subjective, it's something you need to be aware of. Do an online search in the guise of a prospective employer on your own name (using inverted commas to narrow down searches on your name only 'John Smith' home town, etc).

If you wouldn't want your mother to see what you have posted, would you want an employer to see the same content? Whilst you are entitled to your views and opinions, you have the right to remain silent. You do not have to say anything but it may harm your defence if you do not answer when questioned something which you rely on in Court and anything you do say may be given in evidence (as the police say). Employers want to see you using common sense.

Before the Interview

Fail to prepare, prepare to fail is the motto to live by here and it's essential that you do your due diligence and discreetly on the individuals who are going to be leading it.

It's worth doing anonymous searches on LinkedIn to see the background of those who will be conducting the interviews so you can see how long they have been in their respective roles and to show evidence that you have done your homework in the course of the ongoing conversation.

Before you even set off for the interview, it's worth doing a 'dry run' to ensure you know where the office is so you can arrive unflustered and prepared on the day.

This is the checklist I adhere to;

- clean shoes (it's the first thing an interviewer notices)
- pen, paper, CV, list of questions to ask and a crib sheet to refresh your memory on the organisation and the names of the interviewers
- copy of the job specification
- passport, utility bill or bank statement issued within the past 3 months and proof of right to work (HMRC tax code with NI number on it or something similar)
- umbrella
- loose change for bus fares, parking fares and refreshments
- fully charged mobile phone (put on silent upon arrival)

I am always curious to know how the position has come about, and this is a question you can ask either during the interview or in the closing questions. There's no harm in actually trying to find out by either asking someone 'in the know', or through

Google searches to see how often the role has been advertised in the past or simply by trusting your gut instinct.

Always take a copy of your CV with you in a folder with some writing paper, a pen and some questions to close at the end and have this laid out in front of you from the outset to illustrate that you are well prepared and mean business.

Think of examples where you have displayed the competencies in question that are relevant for the job you are being interviewed for. Prepare beforehand and have as many examples as possible so you can convey this at the interview. You may find it useful to pencil in some keywords and prompts against various roles on your CV so you can quickly respond to the popular questions.

You are the solution they are seeking to address their problems, so know your worth and lay it on the line with confidence and no waffle. This is your closing point at the end of the interview, although I have slotted it in here because you need to have this prepared before the interview to complete the circle.

Negative factors to watch for

Your potential employer will be evaluating your negative factors as well as your positive attributes, and the following points are generally considered to be the most frequent aspects that lead to rejection;

- poor personal appearance
- overbearing, aggressive or conceited 'superiority complex' and a 'know it all' demeanour
- inability to clearly express your thoughts or grammar
- lack of planning for career with no purpose or goals
- lack of interest and enthusiasm demonstrated by being passive and indifferent
- lack of confidence and nervousness
- over-emphasis on the remuneration
- evasive answers and excuses for unfavourable elements in your CV
- lack of tact, maturity and courtesy
- condemnation of past employers
- lack of eye contact
- limp handshake
- persistent attitude of 'what can you do for me?'
- lack of preparation for the interview and a failure to know the background about the organisation

The Interview

There are two styles of interviews as far as my experience goes, and that is the private sector and the public sector.

Private sector and public sector interviews usually follow the same 'competency based' theme and format with questions revolving around the STAR acronym, which stands for 'Situation, Task, Action, Result'. You are meant to describe a situation you found yourself in, the task you were asked to do, the action you took and the result at the end of it.

Before any interview begins it's the introduction that sets the scene, and a good handshake, a genuine smile, a friendly disposition and a relaxed manner is pivotal to whether you will succeed. Body language is key and this is how you are judged before the interview commences. You are initially judged on your non-verbal communication before you get out of the starter blocks and first impressions count, so put your best foot forward with a smile, a firm and decent handshake, confidence, don't talk too much and pre-empt some of the answers.

Clear, effective verbal communication remains paramount in today's workplace and solid verbal communication can help us become more productive and build more effective working relationships.

I simply see it as a sales pitch whereby the employer has a problem and I am the solution and answer to it, which takes the pressure off and puts me in the driving seat.

What is a competency?

A competency is a specific quality, knowledge, skill or behaviour a person should have to be successful in a position.

Competencies are personality traits that are exhibited in everything we do, and they can be anything from ability to prioritising to team working.

Why use competency-based interviewing?

This standard approach to screening, selecting and interviewing is designed to help ensure that the selection procedure is objective and fair.

Competency-based interviewing (CBI) is used to dig deeper than ordinary standard interview techniques. It works on the basis of how your past behaviour will depict what your future behaviour will be. You are therefore expected to call upon specific examples from your past experiences to highlight the competencies the interviewer is looking for.

How might a competency-based interview differ from other interviews?

Rather than using the CV or application form as the basis for the interview, it will be structured around a number of competencies, each with its own set of questions. As you move through the questions, the interviewer(s) will take you through what each question is asking and the information being sought.

This information will require you to refer to your past experiences within / outside work and will revolve around your own actions and learning points.

These interviews are designed to show the interviewer(s) how you can fulfil the job in question. The prime concern is to find out as much as possible about your qualities. You can take notes to your interview and will be encouraged to take time to consider your answers before giving them. You may also jump back to previous questions if you remember a point you feel is relevant.

Core Competencies

You will be asked questions on the following competencies as a minimum:

1. Job Knowledge
2. Respect for Diversity
3. Service Delivery
4. Problem Solving
5. Communication
6. Personal Effectiveness

Job Knowledge is self-explanatory, and you obviously need to know what the job entails and align your preparation to it.

Respect for Diversity and Equality is key to the Police Force as you will be dealing with people from all walks of life with different religions, beliefs and standards.

You need to pay particular attention to this as it features as the top priority for police recruitment, given the world we live in.

The police are continually in the public gaze and scrutiny by politicians and everyone, so you need to craft some good answers based on your own personal experience that are aligned to what the police expect to see.

Equality includes the following objectives:

Increase awareness and reporting around hate crime and incidents and provide victims with appropriate support.

Improve engagement with vulnerable or disadvantaged people, particularly young people, to prevent them from becoming either a victim of perpetrator of crime and anti-social behaviour.

Improve service delivery processes to victims of crime who are of Black Minority Ethnicity (BME) as well as victims of gender-based crime such as domestic abuse and serious sexual offences.

Work with partners to raise awareness of the impact of homophobic bullying and the additional risks and vulnerabilities faced by children, young people and the wider community.

Improve access to information and police services for people with a disability as a victim, witness or offender.

You need to think of examples where you have embraced respect and a desire to accommodate the needs of those that fall in to this sphere.

Service Delivery

Delivering a top-tier service to the public is paramount, so you need to think of examples where you have gone above and beyond what is expected of you in previous roles.

I would suggest thinking of examples which did not fit within your job remit, as that is one question that was posed to me and is expected by the police given that no two days are ever the same.

Problem Solving

Being able to think creatively to solve problems is a key aspect of policing as the public rely on the police to do this as part of their jobs. You need to think of unique examples from previous roles in your working life to stand out on this competency.

Communication

You need to be able to demonstrate your ability to clearly explain and articulate yourself to anyone in any role within the police force, so have your answers well rehearsed for the competencies that you are going to be measured against.

Personal Effectiveness

Personal effectiveness involves taking personal responsibility for achieving results to required ethical standards and driving through results from start to finish.

You need to think of examples where you have demonstrated motivation, commitment, perseverance and integrity.

This needs to be aligned to how you plan, manage and organise your own work to effectively achieve organisational goals.

An interviewer will be looking at questions that address the following aspects;

- team-working
- ability to prioritise
- ability to work under pressure and to tight deadlines
- working to targets
- desire to succeed and tenacity
- planning and organising
- communication
- motivation
- personal organisation
- action orientated / achievement orientated
- analytical / problem solving
- initiative
- interpersonal
- adaptability

- client focus
- communication
- problem solving and judgement
- results orientation
- developing others
- impact and influence
- innovation
- leadership
- relationship building
- attention to detail
- conflict management

That may sound daunting but in reality, your CV has opened the door here and the interviewers know that you have the potential to succeed in this role otherwise they wouldn't have invited you to an interview.

Think carefully about motivations and values as you are likely to be asked questions around what your primary motivation is for applying for this role. Your values need to be aligned to Police Scotland's values, so think of examples based on your previous work history to align your answers to the competencies and how you are measured on your responses.

You can expect the interviewers to open the conversation by providing a brief outline of the role and how it has come about.

The opening question you can expect is, *"Can you talk me through your CV and where you are at now"*. You need to know your CV inside out hence having a copy in front of you as a back-stop so you can't fluff the interview before you start.

Behavioural Competencies

Each of these competencies are assigned to the seniority of the role that you are applying for.

The three grades are as follows:

Essential
Supervisory
Management

I have focused on the essential criteria as this is the minimum that is expected from you on each aspect of the interview.

The Competent Indicator examples are what you are expected to demonstrate to pass each aspect of the interview.

These are based on principals of Association of Chief Police Officers in Scotland Performance and Development Review Behaviour Descriptors.

The behavioural competencies are as follows:

Respect for Diversity

__Respects, values and considers__ the opinions, circumstances, feelings and views of colleagues and members of the public, taking into account their diverse backgrounds.

Is tactful and diplomatic when dealing with people, treating them with dignity and respect at all times. ***Understands and is sensitive to social, cultural and racial differences and needs.***

Competent Indicator examples

- Identifies and respects other peoples' values or opinions

- Acknowledges and respects the broad range of social or cultural customs and beliefs

- Challenges inappropriate behaviour and attitudes which are abusive, aggressive or discriminatory

- Is polite, tolerant and patient, treating all with dignity and respect

- Listens and understands the needs and interests of others

- Uses appropriate language and behaviour and is sensitive to how these may affect people

- Respects confidentiality, when appropriate

Effective Communication

Communicates ideas and information effectively, both verbally and in writing. Uses appropriate language and a style of communication that is relevant to the situation and people being addressed.

Capable of persuading and influencing others in a variety of situations.

Competent Indicator examples

- Speaks clearly and concisely

- Communicates information and instructions confidently and in an appropriate style

- Uses correct spelling, punctuation and grammar

- Listens carefully

- Summarises information to check people understand it

- Makes sure communication has a clear purpose, is factual and accurate, and provided at the right time

- Pays attention and shows interest in what others are saying

- Records relevant information and includes the salient points in written notes/reports

- Seeks clarity when uncertain about information or instruction

- Influences people or situations through effective communication

Job Knowledge

Demonstrates a *sound working knowledge* **within current role. Understands what other areas of the organisation do in order to operate effectively.**

Utilises specialist training in an operational or practical setting. **Demonstrates a willingness to learn and keep knowledge up to date.**

Competent Indicator examples

- Demonstrates a sound working knowledge of all legislation, policies and procedures relevant to current role

- Understands and adheres to legislation, policies and procedures relevant to their role

- Continually keeps updated on changes in legislation, policies and procedures

- Is willing to learn new skills and put them into practice

- Shares knowledge and experience with others, where appropriate

- Seeks ways to improve own learning and self-development

Leadership

Leads by example *and is a role model to others.*

Competent Indicator examples

- Steps forward to lead as needed

- Understands the importance of having a strong sense of purpose and common goal

- Is thoughtful, fair and leads by example

- Demonstrates a 'do the right thing' attitude

- Demonstrates common sense and sound judgement

- Gives clear and concise instructions

- Is trusted by members of the team

- Considers the thoughts and opinions of others

- Considers the moral and ethical consequences of actions

Management Ability

Looks at issues with a **broad view.** *Acts in the best interests of the organisation as a whole, rather than just own area or department.*

Thinks ahead *and prepares for the future.* **Plans, organises and manages work activities,** *ensuring that resources are used effectively and efficiently to achieve organisational goals.*

Competent Indicator examples

- Steps forward to lead as needed

- Understands the importance of having a strong sense of purpose and common goal

- Is thoughtful, fair and leads by example
- Demonstrates a 'do the right thing' attitude
- Demonstrates common sense and sound judgement
- Gives clear and concise instructions
- Is trusted by members of the team
- Considers the thoughts and opinions of others
- Considers the moral and ethical consequences of actions

Partnership Working

Recognises the importance of partnership working and consultation. Establishes and **maintains effective relationships with partner agencies** *to maximise the potential of a* **joint problem-solving approach.**

Competent Indicator examples

- Represents the service in an appropriate and professional manner
- Encourages and develops a shared problem-solving approach with partner agencies
- Works effectively as a team member of a multi-agency, multi-disciplinary team
- Establishes, maintains and utilises relationships with relevant partner agencies
- Adheres to organisational policies that outline the responsibilities when working with other partners
- Shares information appropriately with partnership agencies

- Ensures colleagues and line management are kept informed of activities, as appropriate

Personal Awareness

Recognises how **feelings and emotions** *affect their own performance and how this may impact on others.*

Handles difficult or sensitive situations *with empathy and diplomacy.*

Competent Indicator examples

- Recognises how feelings and emotions affect their own performance and how this may impact on others

- Listens well, shows sensitivity and empathy to others' views, needs and feelings

- Shows interest in others and builds trust and confidence

- Is able to show a sense of humour and flexibility, where appropriate

- Shows confidence in their own abilities

Personal Effectiveness

Takes **personal responsibility** *for making things happen and achieving results to required standards. Displays motivation, commitment, perseverance,* **integrity** *and acts in an ethical way.*

Plans, organises *and manages own work to effectively achieve organisational goals.*

Is reliable and **resilient**, *even in difficult circumstances. Recognises the need for* **change** *and is willing to adapt.*

Competent Indicator examples

- Understands how own role contributes to achieving organisational goals

- Manages personal time well, is able to prioritise, achieve results and meet deadlines

- Sets own realistic objectives and achieves consistent and effective work performance on time and to the required standard

- Works with minimal supervision when needed but is not afraid to ask for advice when facing new challenges or when clarification is required

- Maintains high personal and professional standards

- Is punctual, reliable and keen

- Has a positive attitude towards change

- Is willing to take on new or different responsibilities or change roles

- Understands and uses new technology to improve performance

Problem Solving

*Gathers information from a range of sources to **identify problems** draws logical conclusions and makes **effective decisions.***

*Can **initiate new ideas** when required.*

Competent Indicator examples

- Works within tried and tested procedures and remains focused on the main issues

- Identifies inconsistencies in information

- Effectively uses resources to resolve issues

- Assesses situations, verifies critical information, considers options and draws logical conclusions

- Assesses the effect and impact of decisions

- Remains calm, impartial and avoids jumping to conclusions

- Demonstrates sound judgement and can make and justify decisions

- Takes a course of action within appropriate timescales

- Accepts responsibility for decisions and learns from mistakes

- Can be creative when required

- Gathers and makes appropriate use of evidence or information

- Uses previous knowledge and experience to best advantage

Service Delivery

Focuses on the individual **needs and concerns of the customer** *and responds accordingly with* **a high quality service**. *Maintains contact and updates as appropriate.*

Competent Indicator examples

- Presents an appropriate image

- Supports organisational strategies that serve the customer

- Deals with customer complaints within a reasonable time

- Aims to deliver agreed targets on time

- Responds and prioritises customer requests, taking account of other work demands

- Ensures customers receive the best service possible and are made to feel valued

- Manages customer expectations

- Keeps customers updated on progress

- Listens and learns from relevant customer feedback

Team Working

Develops **strong working relationships** *inside and outside the team to achieve common goals. Communicates within groups and considers others in discussions and decisions.* **Actively helps and supports others.**

Competent Indicator examples

- Actively takes part in team tasks in the workplace

- Is open and approachable, taking others views into account and valuing their contribution

- Forms productive working relationships with colleagues

- Asks for and accepts help when needed

- Provides guidance and support to new team members

- Develops mutual trust and confidence in others

- Is loyal to members of the team and decisions

- Takes on unpopular or routine tasks

- Co-operates with and supports others, sharing knowledge and experience

Popular Questions

These are the questions I was asked for the criteria I was measured against for an administrative role.

Problem Solving – Can you give me an example where you have had to solve a problem and what you did to address it?

Situation – I spoke about my first book that I wrote where I scrutinised 7 pieces of legislation based on a lifetime of personal consumer and motoring experiences that I have resolved alone.

Task – I created templates based on real life examples that are tried and tested and can be used in various common scenarios.

Action – I completed this book within 3 months and wrote 40,000 words to capture legislation such as the Consumer Rights Act 2015 and the Misrepresentation Act 1967 which is available on Amazon, and I created a popular consumer website to link to it which has over 100 blogs based on current consumer matters that will create mini-books later this year.

Result – As above + my book has plenty of 5* reviews on Amazon to evidence that it what I have written has helped others resolve similar problems.

Answers don't have to be work-related, although you are obviously expected to link an answer to a scenario that is work-related and you need to have a well-rehearsed answer here describing the scenario and problem, what you suggested as a solution, how you enacted it and the outcome.

One question you can expect and need to be prepared for is, ***"What particular contribution do you consider that you bring to this role?"***.

A solid answer to this would be along the lines of;

- effective people management skills
- clarity of thought
- attention to detail and a keen sense of the importance of quality service to internal and external stakeholders
- a solid education coupled with a variety and depth of work experience that has equipped me to deal with many different scenarios
- common sense and the ability to 'hit the ground running' and learn new things quickly

Service Delivery / Personal Effectiveness – Can you give me an example where you have had to take on a task that you have been asked to do that is not within your remit and job description?

Situation – I was working in a team of 10 on an assignment in Manchester with various nationalities, creeds and cultures where we had to liaise with Relationship Managers ("RMs") and clients as part of our collective remit to complete our 'Know Your Customer' project as (a bank) had 1.3m corporate customers that they didn't quite know the full picture of.

Task – My Team Manager quickly gathered that writing is my forte and asked me to help others in the team in crafting e-mails to RMs to fill in the gaps that we identified to complete our understanding of their customers.

Action – I worked with others in the team to polish their e-mails and reword as necessary to positively engage with the RMs and build a relationship with them. They could then liaise with their clients to enable us to quickly complete our understanding and close the case.

Result – I was able to work with others in the team to do just that so my Team Manager could focus on more important matters. He took that in to account in readjusting his expectations on my own output.

Can you give me an example where you have had to drive through an improvement and how it evolved?

Situation – I was part of a team of 12 individuals of various ages and experience and our work was flowing in from India to varying degrees of quality.

Task – Our remit was to read the reports, tidy them up and decide whether the suspicions for Money Laundering were genuine and to either disclose it to the National Crime Agency ('NCA') or close it.

A lot of the cases that were coming from India were rejected because an incorrect decision was made due to a lack of understanding and awareness.

Action – I took part in fortnightly conference calls with my Team Manager and another colleague with the Team Leaders in India to discuss trends and common themes to address the issues.

Result – We saw a 57% improvement on the rejection rates of work within 4 weeks. Our colleagues in India appreciated our feedback, coaching and engagement. Morale improved in India and Edinburgh based on a rapid improvement of the quality of work being processed.

Difficult Situations – can you give me an example where you have had to deal with a difficult situation with a colleague and how you handled it?

Situation – I spoke about the two Directors and co-owners of the business who simply fell out and were sat on different floors while I was the sole administrator tasked with dealing with their clients.

They were not on speaking terms and the post was coming in on the Ground Floor to one Director. The other Director on the First Floor was not timely receiving it and neither was I, which resulted in clients complaining about not getting a timely response.

Task – I took it upon myself to meet with both Directors and explain that I was getting grief from their customers about not getting timely responses to their queries and correspondence, which was affecting their business and my ability to deliver and meet our SLAs.

Action – We agreed that the post would come in and be stamped, timed and initialled by one Director on the Ground Floor. I would collect it and hand it to another Director to do the same and pass to me within an agreed timeframe so I could act on it and provide a timely response to our clients.

Result – It resolved the problem and I was able to meet the clients' needs and expectations.

If you can't recall anything specific from your CV, feel free to say so but elaborate by saying that you would try to find some common ground and understand why they feel the way they do. Say that you would take a non-confrontational style without involving management, you are both working for the same employer that shares the same objectives and desire to succeed and seek any suggestions and ideas from them to break the deadlock.

A good example that could never be questioned would be to describe a **situation** whereby you were working in a small office / team with a more junior team member who had a reputation for not pulling their weight.

The **task** you were faced with is that you were finding it difficult to get the most out of him and you found yourself thinking back to what your colleagues had said about the individual.

The **action** you chose was to speak to him informally and in private and give him some feedback on what the general consensus was within the team and office. You did this in a diplomatic way asking if he needed more guidance or if he was having any trouble at all.

The **result** is that he opened up saying he was not aware of how we was perceived by the team, that he sometimes did not understand what he was meant to be doing and that other senior team members had taken over the assignments without involving or coaching him. He found it difficult to speak up.

I took this on board and dedicated extra time to assisting him with our tasks as well as giving him more (guided) responsibility. I also spoke to my senior colleagues and asked them to be aware of more junior staff concerns. His work improved and he felt much happier within the team.

Another response would be to simply say that I aim to treat everyone fairly whether it's an internal or external stakeholder and I welcome different points of view in trying to ascertain the best way forward in the interests of the business. I find it interesting to hear how different people see things and that it's a great learning opportunity.

This answer can also be spun in a similar vein to dealing with conflicts in the workplace.

Diversity and Equality – can you give me an example where you have had to embrace diversity and equality and what you did?

Situation – I spoke about the fact that we had a few Muslims in the workplace and that it's prayer time on a Friday lunchtime, where we would try and use the First Aid Room for that purpose.

Sometimes it wasn't possible to do so as it was in use.

Task – On occasions where it wasn't in use, I would have to quickly identify other solutions to address and embrace their needs and requirements.

Action – I would occasionally lend them my pass so they could use the Loading Bay and discreetly liaise with delivery drivers so they could not be disturbed and make other arrangements to take in deliveries.

Result – It worked well and it's a good example of engaging with others of different cultures, beliefs and creeds and respecting and addressing their needs and requirements.

Closing questions

These are the questions you can expect once you're on the home straight, and the current trend seems to be for interviewers to ask, *"What three words would your friends / colleagues use to describe you?"*.

They seem to think they are throwing a curveball here, and the answers you need to recite are;

1. friendly (indicates you are a good team player)

2. conscientious (they can never spell that but they love to hear it)
3. integrity (this is your fallback position if the job goes pear-shaped and you need to take the high ground)

Recite those answers and you will have neatly covered that off.

Another popular one at the time of writing this is, *"What would you say is your proudest achievement in your career?"*. You are expected to make this work-related as the question is designed to link your highlights with the job description, but this question is subjective and can be interpreted in different ways.

Personally, I like to home in on my writing and finding a passion I never knew I had by virtue of writing a travel blog that was subsequently published by the Shetland Islands Tourist Board and facilitated a private invite to the Up Helly Aa Viking Fire Festival. It's true, it cannot be doubted or questioned and it's an answer that won't easily be forgotten.

I then elaborate by chatting about the first book I wrote and self-published, the popular consumer website I created which attracts a lot of global traffic and guest blogs that I occasionally write for other publishers, writers and the tourism industry.

Interviewers love a good storyteller so have your yarns ready and watertight so they cannot be questioned or doubted, as rest assured, they will be doing Google searches afterwards to verify what you have said.

Questions you ask to close

You need to have some solid questions to hand to close the interview off, and this is your golden opportunity to turn the tables and start doing some digging to find out if this organisation is all it's cracked up to be. Some of my favourites are;

Do you have any concerns about my ability to do this role?

The way the interviewers respond to this question will give you a good indication as to whether you have it in the bag or not. Occasionally, you can expect a question revolving around team work or prioritising your work, but it's rare that you will get caught out here.

How would you describe the culture of the team and organisation?

This is pivotal to me as you need to try and gauge how the team ticks and how the organisation operates, and the way this question is answered will give you a good indication about whether this is the right fit for you. If the interviewers are cagey about different personalities and characters within the team and organisation, you can be assured this is a pig in a poke.

Any mention of the word 'traditional' is one to be wary of as this tells me that the firm is stuck in the dark ages, is resistant and does not easily embrace change and is full of dead wood that wouldn't survive anywhere else.

What is the best thing you would say about working here?

This is always an interesting question to ask and how this is handled by your interviewers will tell you more in less than 10 seconds than the whole interview process. If the interviewers stare blankly at each other and start waffling on about free fruit and 'dress down Friday', you know that you are looking at a pig in a poke. Likewise, if they keep reciting about nobody ever leaving and staff longevity, it's another red flag to me. The place is probably full of lazy, dead wood that doesn't know any different and are resigned to the fact that this is as good as it gets with no chance of being able to make any meaningful difference regardless of the yarn that has been fed to you.

A passionate, sincere response aligned with your own values is a sign that you are on to a good thing.

I am seeking an organisation that can offer opportunities and longevity, and I would like to ask what has kept you here for so long?

It's a valid question to ask and one that no interviewer would expect to be asked, so it's one to consider. There is a lot to be said for longevity and loyalty with any employer, but equally, we all know that there is no such thing nowadays whether it's sticking with an employer, a utility firm or a service provider.

Loyalty doesn't pay and is rarely rewarded, so why has the interviewer stuck with this outfit for so long? More often than not, it's simply due to inertia and the fact that these individuals are just dead wood who couldn't survive anywhere else or are reluctant to step out of their comfort zone.

Ask the question and see what answer you get to gauge your gut instinct.

How has this role come about?

This is another one to treat with caution as yarns flow both ways. The interviewer is hardly going to be honest and say that they can't find anyone with the staying power to put up with the rubbish that comes with the role.

I recall one boss saying to me that the last incumbent held the role for about 5 years and moved on to pastures new but failed to say that the one after that only lasted 4 weeks and he passed that off after I accepted the role as a temporary worker. No doubt he will spin the same yarn to the unfortunate soul who has taken the role I binned after 3 months as a temporary worker as well.

Do your homework on this and don't be afraid to 'call them out' if you doubt the authenticity of their response, albeit subtly. I recall an opening line being said to me by a law firm that this was a new role due to expansion, yet I responded by saying that I find that curious as I seem to recall applying for this position on more than one occasion in the past as I have been keen to work for such a well-respected firm. They fluffed and waffled and even admitted that they thought they recognised my name and CV, and that set the scene for me to storm the interview with brass balls and confidence knowing that I had caught them out in the early stages before we even got in to our stride.

The closing question from them was, *"Do you have any holidays planned?"*. My answer, with a cheeky smile and wink at the girl asking the question, was, *"Yes, I am off to Spain for Christmas if you fancy carrying my bag"*. She gave me a cheeky wink on the way out and said they would be in touch. I am still waiting for the phone call!

Other questions that are worth asking are;

- *What opportunities are there for career progression?*
- *Could you explain to me in what direction the organisation wants to move over the next few years?*
- *What training can I expect to receive for this role?*
- *What do you consider to be the main challenges of the job?*
- *How would you describe the main values of the organisation?*
- *Will the organisation provide opportunity for professional qualifications?*
- *Is there anything that you would like to improve in your department?*
- *What development plans does the organisation have?*
- *What is your personal experience of working for this organisation?*
- ***Will*** *there be opportunities for developing my role?*
- *How **will** my success be measured in this role?*

Note the use of **present tense words** here and not hypothetical words – ie, if you were to be offered the job - to reinforce your interest and desire to secure the job.

Finally, thank the interviewer for their time and consideration in meeting you, always delivered with a smile and sincerity.

If you have conveyed;

- why you are interested in the job and organisation
- what you can offer and your ability to do the job

your work is done and you have done the best you can.

After the Interview

The jury is out for me as to whether you send a 'thank you' e-mail to the interviewer afterwards to convey your appreciation for the time they took to meet you and that you remain interested in the role.

I haven't had any success with this technique in Scotland if truth be known. I seem to think that it's a cultural thing in Scotland to be reticent with your enthusiasm and desire to 'put yourself forward' over and above everyone else.

Some agencies and recruiters recommend it, although I think it depends on the job market and culture of the area you are working in.

It's your call, but it's one I am wary of, knowing that it hasn't worked for me.

Nevertheless, if you have used a recruiter as a conduit for the role that you have applied for, the first thing you ought to do is ring them to let them know how the interview went and that you are keen (or not) as the case may be.

Useful Contacts

If you believe that there have been breaches regarding the processing of your personal data in an organisation, your first port of call is the Information Commissioner's Office ('ICO') and website where you can clarify any concerns you may have.

UK

The UK's independent authority was set up to uphold information rights in the public interest, promoting openness by public bodies and data privacy for individuals.

Their website holds a wealth of information on Data Protection, the General Data Protection Regulation ('GDPR'), Freedom of Information and register which you can search to see if a Data Controller is registered with the ICO and how to escalate any breaches you believe may have been made.

Information Commissioner's Office
Wycliffe House
Water Lane
Wilmslow
Cheshire
SK9 5AF

Tel: 0303 123 1113 (local rate) or 01625 545 745 if you prefer to use a national rate number.

Scotland

Scotland has its own Information Commissioner who regulates the Freedom for Information (Scotland) Act which covers Scottish public authorities. The main focus of the ICO in Scotland is Data Protection, and the ICO is the sole regulatory body in Scotland for this.

The Information Commissioner's Office – Scotland
45 Melville Street
Edinburgh
EH3 7HL

Tel: 0303 123 1115

Email: scotland@ico.org.uk

Wales

The ICO's office in Cardiff provides a local point of contact for members of the public and organisations based in Wales.

Information Commissioner's Office – Wales
2nd Floor, Churchill House
Churchill Way
Cardiff
CF10 2HH

Tel: 0330 414 6421 to talk to the team.

Email: wales@ico.org.uk

Northern Ireland

The contact details for the ICO in Northern Ireland are as follows;

Information Commissioner's Office
3rd Floor
14 Cromac Place
Belfast
BT7 2JB

Tel: 028 9027 8757 or 0303 123 1114

Email: ni@ico.org.uk

If you believe that any regulatory breaches have taken place within your tenure at a firm that is regulated by the Financial Conduct Authority, you are well within your rights to contact the regulator who will have an individual and team assigned to manage that firm's relationship and provide oversight.

This would fall within the remit of whistleblowing and the regulator is duty bound to investigate any concerns. This would be made in tandem with the firm's internal Compliance and Regulatory functions, and you may struggle to get any independent answers or to hold anyone to account simply because the firm's internal oversight isn't an independent function and colludes with those involved to protect the firm's reputation.

Regulated Financial Institutions
The Financial Conduct Authority
25 The North Colonnade
London
E14 5HS

Tel: 0207 066 1000

W: www.fca.org.uk

The Citizens Advice Bureau can offer assistance and guidance on any employment matters, although it's worth bearing in mind that the law differs across the UK and you will have to direct your concerns and queries via your local office within your residential jurisdiction.

Their website is www.citizensadvice.org.uk and you can find the most popular topics on their site within the past month in addition to guidance on employment matters and any other relevant concerns you may have encountered.

Connect with the Author

Want to stay in touch with Scott and be the first to hear about his new books?

Social media links:

Instagram: @grumpy_g1t

Twitter: @grumpy_g1t

Facebook: The Complaints Resolver

Websites:

www.awriterinedinburgh.com

www.thegrumpygit.com

If you enjoyed this book, don't forget to leave a review on Amazon! I highly appreciate your reviews, and it only takes a minute to do.

Printed in Great Britain
by Amazon

86037981R00027